Acknowledgements
Jarrold Publishing Ltd would like to thank all those who kindly gave
permission to reproduce the words and visual material in this book:
copyright holders have been identified where possible and we apologise
for any inadvertent omissions.

We would particularly like to thank Sheldrake Press for the use of pictures
from the Victorian Cookbook and The Shorter Mrs Beeton.

First published in Great Britain in 1998
Jarrold Publishing Ltd
Whitefriars, Norwich NR3 1TR

Developed and produced by
Ivor Claydon/Graphics
Researched and edited by David Notley
Printed and bound in Spain 1/98
Copyright© 1998 Jarrold Publishing Ltd

EQUATION
LABOUR LIGHT, CLOTHES WHITE BY SUNLIGHT.

Victorian
RECIPES

JARROLD PUBLISHING

Contents

Clear Mulligatawny Soup

4 large onions
2 cooking apples
50g/2oz butter
Bunch of fresh herbs
1 tablespoon curry powder
Juice of 1 lemon
1 tablespoon chutney
6 cardamoms
2 black peppercorns
3.3 litres/6 pints stock
Roast game or poultry bones.

Peel and cut onions and cooking apples in very thin slices, put them into a stewpan with the butter and herbs, fry for twenty minutes; then mix with the curry powder, lemon juice, chutney, cardamoms, pounded black peppercorns, stock and the roast game or poultry bones; bring to the boil, then skim and allow the stock to cook gently for about one hour; then strain and remove the fat, and clarify; strain off

through a clean soup cloth, and return to the bain marie to get hot. Serve with diced pieces of cooked game or poultry in the tureen. You can serve this with a plate of boiled rice, or just Indian breads that are readily available now.
Time 2 hours/Serves 12

Oxtail Soup

2 oxtails cut into pieces
2 slices of ham
25g/1oz of butter
2 carrots and 2 turnips
3 onions
1 leek and 1 head of celery
Bunch of fresh herbs, parsley, thyme and bayleaf
12 whole peppercorns
4 cloves
1 tablespoonful of salt
2 tablespoonfuls of tomato ketchup
$^1/_2$ glass of port
3.3 litres/6 pints of water
A little flour and butter to thicken

Trim and wash the oxtails and put them in a stewpan with the butter. Cut the vegetables in slices and add them to a stewpan with the ham, peppercorns, spices and herbs. Put in 300ml/$^1/_2$ pint of water, and vigorously stir on a high heat for 10 minutes. Fill up the stewpan with the water and, when boiling, add the salt. Skim well, and simmer gently for about 4 hours, or until the tails are tender. Take them out, skim and strain the soup, thicken with a little flour worked together with butter, and flavour with the ketchup and port. Put back the tails, simmer for 5 minutes and serve.
Time 4 hours/Serves 12

Green Pea Soup

675g/1¹/₂lbs of shelled green peas
100g/4oz butter
2-3 thin slices of ham
6 onions sliced
4 shredded lettuces
1¹/₂ teacupfuls of fresh breadcrumbs
225g/8oz spinach
¹/₂ teaspoonful of sugar
1.1 litres/2 pints of medium stock

Put the butter, ham, two-thirds of the shelled peas, the onions and lettuces into a stewpan with 600ml/1 pint of the stock and simmer for 1 hour; then add the remainder of the stock, with the breadcrumbs and boil for another hour. Now boil the spinach and squeeze it very dry. Rub the soup through a sieve, and the spinach with it, to colour it. Have ready the rest of the peas, boiled; add them to the soup, put in the sugar; give one boil and serve. If necessary, add salt.
Time 2 hours/Serves 6

Potage Printanier, or Spring Soup

225g/8oz of shelled green peas
A little chervil
2 shredded lettuces
2 onions
A very small bunch of parsley
50g/2oz of butter
3 egg yolks
600ml/1 pint of water
Seasoning to taste
2.2 litres/4 pints of medium stock

Put in a clean stewpan the peas, chervil, lettuces, onions, parsley and butter, with the water and let them simmer till tender. Season with salt and pepper. When done, strain off the vegetables, and add two-thirds of the liquor they were boiled in to the stock. Beat up the yolks of the eggs with the other third, give it a toss over the heat, and at the moment of serving, add this, with the vegetables which you strained off, to the soup.
Time ³/4 hour/Serves 8

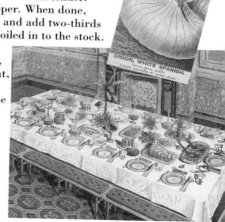

Spanish Chestnut Soup

350g/12oz of Spanish chestnuts
150ml/¹/4 pint of cream
Seasoning to taste of salt, cayenne and mace
1.1 litre/2 pints of medium stock

Put the chestnuts into a large pan of warm water. As soon as this becomes too hot for the fingers to remain in it, take out the chestnuts, peel them quickly, immerse them in water, and wipe and weigh them. Now cover them with some of the stock, and stew them gently for rather more than an hour, or until they break when touched with a fork; then drain, pound and rub them through a fine sieve. Add the rest of the stock, mace, cayenne and salt, and stir it often until it boils, take it off the heat and put in the cream.
Time 1¹/2 hours/Serves 6

Mayonnaise of Chicken in Shells

1 jar of thick mayonnaise sauce
450g/1lb cold chicken
Crisp lettuce
6 hard-boiled egg
225g/8oz chicken livers
25g/1oz butter
Pepper and salt
Fillets of boned anchovies
100g/4oz stoned olives
Tarragon and chervil or parsley
French capers
1 jar French gherkin or beetroot

Have china or plated scallop shells for these; place about one teaspoonful of thick mayonnaise in the centre of each shell; take the remains of cold chicken and cut it in little neat pieces, also little crisp pieces of lettuce and slices of four hard-boiled eggs, fillets of anchovies and olives. Arrange these alternately on the sauce, forming a nice pile, then cover with mayonnaise sauce and smooth the top with a knife. Fry the chicken livers in a little butter for about ten minutes and season with a little pepper and salt; rub the livers, when cool, through a wire sieve, then sprinkle over the mayonnaise. Take the hard-boiled yolk of 2 eggs, pass them through the sieve and lightly sprinkle on the liver, adding a little chopped tarragon and chervil or parsley. Place four little bunches of capers on the edge of the mayonnaise, on top of each coquille put two neat fillets of anchovies, with a little strip of gherkin or beetroot between the fillets and serve.
Time 1 hour/Serves 10

Breast of Duckling with Oranges

4 duck breasts
Potatoes
Bigarade sauce

Fry the duck breasts for 20 minutes in a hot pan with a little olive oil. Remove the duck breasts and cut in nice neat slices; arrange the compote of oranges in the centre of a white plate, with a creamed potato border and serve the sliced fillets on top. Serve with a Bigarade sauce by deglazing a wineglass of sherry, juice of one lemon and one orange in the juices of the pan. Add 150ml/^{1}/$_4$ pint of water, a little sugar some very finely cut orange peel and boil vigorously and reduce the sauce by half. Pour a little of the Bigarade sauce over the finished dish and serve.

COMPOTE OF ORANGES

4 oranges
Water
Pinch of caster sugar

Peel the oranges, divide them into their natural divisions, remove the pips and skin, and warm over boiling water between two plates, adding a pinch of castor sugar.
Time 1 hour/Serves 4

Terrine of Rabbit

900g/2lbs of fresh rabbit meat, boned, the rabbit's liver
225g/8oz of fresh pork
50g/2oz of belly of pork
100g/4oz of lean raw bacon
1 onion finely chopped
2 cloves of garlic
Salt and pepper
Spices: a good pinch of mace and nutmeg
Water

Put all the ingredients through a mincing-machine or food processor and season with salt, pepper and spices; then put the ingredients into a terrine. Place the terrine into a bain marie or a tin, pour in the boiling water to within 25mm/1 inch of the top of the terrine. Bring to the boil again on top of the stove, then put it quickly into a hot oven 210° C (425°F or Mark 7). The time of cooking may be judged by allowing 35 minutes for every 450g/1lb of the contents of the terrine, but it is better not to rely entirely on time. When you think the terrine should be cooked, take off the cover and push a skewer into the middle of the meat. If this comes out burning hot through its whole length, the terrine is done. Cover the terrine and leave to get cold, do not touch it until the next day. It is then ready to be eaten when it is quite cold. Take it out of the terrine, trim it and serve with a little green salad, bread and, if you wish, a tomato and mango chutney.
Time 2 hours/Serves 10-12

Chicken Croquettes

50-75g/2-3oz chicken
Salt and pepper
50g/2oz chopped ham
1 dessertspoonful of cornflour
150ml/^{1}/4 pint milk
225g/8oz flour
50g/2oz lard
Water
1 egg yolk
Vermicelli or brown breadcrumbs
Parsley

Mince the chicken and season with salt and pepper, adding the chopped ham. Put the cornflour into a basin and make it into a smooth paste with the milk. Put it into a saucepan, and stir until it just boils. It should be as thick as a good stiff batter. Mix your meat with it, and leave on a plate to cool. Rub the flour and lard together and mix into a stiff dough with a very little cold water. Roll out as thin as a piece of writing-paper. Cut it into small rounds or squares just large enough to hold a teaspoonful of the meat mixture and to double over. Having put the meat on to each piece of dough, wet the edges as little as possible, turn the dough over the meat like a turnover, and press the edges firmly together. Brush each over with the yolk of an egg; sprinkle vermicelli or brown breadcrumbs on the top; fry in boiling lard. Drain well, and serve hot, garnish with parsley and serve with a little green salad.
Time 30 minutes/Serves 4

Mussels on Skewers with Truffles

2-3 dozen fresh mussels
1 onion
Bunch of herbs (thyme, parsley bayleaf)
Black and white peppercorns
Juice of 1 lemon
Pinch of salt
600ml/1 pint of water
300ml/^{1}/2 pint of dry white wine
Finely chopped truffle
Black pepper
Olive oil
Cos or iceberg lettuce
Black and white peppercorns

Take the fresh mussels, wash them well and put them in a stewpan with the onion sliced, add the herbs, black and white peppercorns, lemon juice, and a pinch of salt, add to them the water and white wine, bring to the boil, and then let them simmer for about two or three minutes. Turn out into a basin, leave them till cold, then remove from each the beard, which is the part that is like a little piece of weed; put them on a plate and season them with finely chopped truffle, black pepper, and olive oil. Let them lie in this seasoning for about one hour. Take some skewers and arrange about three or four mussels on each skewer with a slice of truffle between each. Serve on a little crisp finely shredded lettuce and sprinkle with pepper, and serve for hors d'œuvre or savoury.
Time 2 hours/Serves 8-10

Herring Roes à la Varsovie

450g/1lb soft roes of fresh herring
Salt
3-4 laurel leaves
3 tablespoonfuls of white tarragon vinegar
300ml/½ pint of water
8-10 peppercorns
Cucumber
French capers
Salad oil
A little black pepper
Chopped parsley

Take the soft roes, remove all the blood from them, and very carefully wash them in cold salt water; then put them into a pie dish with the laurel leaves. Add the white tarragon vinegar to the boiling water and the peppercorns; boil them up together, then strain on to the roes. Put them in a moderate oven with the dish covered with a piece of buttered or greased paper and let them cook for ten minutes, then remove from the oven and leave till cold. Cut the cucumber into diced shapes, mix with half its bulk of French capers and season well with salad oil. Make a little pile of this on each plate, using about a tablespoonful for each, place one of the prepared roes on the top, sprinkle over with a little black pepper and chopped parsley and serve. This is also nice for a savoury. The liquor from the herring roes can be used several times.
Time 30 minutes/Serves 6-8

Lyons Sausage and Egg

450g/1lb Lyons sausage
4 hard-boiled egg yolks
French gherkin
1 bunch chervil and tarragon

Take some Lyons sausage and cut in thin slices, peeling off the outer skin; allow one slice for each person; have some hard-boiled yolk of egg rubbed through a fine sieve, on each slice of sausage arrange about a teaspoonful of the egg, place a few thinly cut strips of gherkin on top, a few sprigs of fresh herbs, season and place each portion on a small white plate.
Time 20 minutes/Serves 6

Sardines à la Royale

1 tin sardines
Endive leaves
2 tablespoonsful olive oil
Few drops of tarragon vinegar
French gherkin
Hard-boiled white of egg
1 cooked beetroot

Remove the skin from the sardines; with a small knife remove the back bone and close up the fillets again; season little crisp leaves of endive with olive oil and vinegar, place them in the middle of a small plate, put the sardine on the top, and arrange crossways little strips of gherkin and hard-boiled white of egg. Place a little chopped beetroot down the sides of the sardines. Serve as hors-d'œuvre or savoury.
Time 30 minutes/Serves 6

Salmon à la Gourmet

450g/1lb smoked salmon
Olive oil
Lemon juice
Black pepper
6 rock oysters
2 tablespoonsful chopped tarragon and chervil
Brown bread
Butter

Take some smoked salmon, cut it in slices about the 3mm/^{1}/8 inch thick, and roll it up, steep it in olive oil and lemon juice and season with a tiny dust of black pepper. Put it on a small white plate, place a raw native oyster similarly seasoned on the top, and sprinkle with a little chopped tarragon and chervil and a dust of black pepper. Arrange two slices of brown bread and butter on the side of the little plate, and serve. Take new bread for the brown bread and butter, cut it into little squares, and roll it up in cylinder shapes.

Time 30 minutes/Serves 6

Skate Baked with Gruyère

900g/2lb boned skate (fish weighing about 2kg/4¹/2lb)
75-100g/3-4oz butter
600ml/1 pint milk
2 heaped teaspoons cornflour
4 cloves and 2 bouquets garnis
Salt and pepper
4 shallots, finely chopped
12 very small onions, peeled and kept whole
150g/6oz Gruyère cheese, grated
6 thin slices of wholemeal bread

Cut the skate in thick strips and roll them up. Put the fish in a wide pan with 25g/1oz of the butter, the milk mixed with the cornflour, the cloves, bouquets garnis, salt, pepper and chopped shallots. Cover the pan, bring to the boil and simmer for 10 minutes. Meanwhile, spread half the cheese over the bottom of a flattish ovenproof dish and cook the very small onions in a little boiling water until tender, then drain them. Fry the slices of bread in the remaining butter until brown and crisp, then cut each piece into four triangles. Arrange the fried bread around the outside of a serving dish. Lift the rolls of fish from the poaching liquid and lay them over the cheese, interspersed with the onions. Strain the liquid over the fish and sprinkle the remaining cheese on top. Bake the dish at 180°C (350°F or Mark 4) for 20 minutes and brown the top before serving.
Time 1 hour/Serves 6

Fish Pie

450g/1lb of cooked fish, such as cod or haddock
Pepper and salt to taste
225g/8oz breadcrumbs
1/2 teaspoonful of grated nutmeg
1 tablespoonful of finely chopped parsley

Clear the fish from the bones, and put a layer of it in a pie dish, with a sprinkle of pepper and salt, then with a layer of breadcrumbs, nutmeg, and chopped parsley. Repeat this till the dish is quite full. You may form a covering either of breadcrumbs, which should be browned, or puff pastry, which should be cut into long strips and laid in cross-bars over the fish, with a line of the pastry first laid round the edge. Before putting the top on, pour in some melted butter, or a little white sauce and bake in a hot oven for 20 minutes. Time 40 minutes/Serves 4

Baked Turbot

4 turbot cutlets
1 egg
100g/4oz breadcrumbs
Cayenne and salt to taste
Minced parsley
Pinch of nutmeg
Juice of 1 lemon
100g/4oz butter

After having cleared the fish from all skin and bone, divide it into square pieces of an equal size; brush them over with egg, and sprinkle with breadcrumbs mixed with a little minced parsley and seasoning. Lay the fish in a baking dish, with sufficient butter to baste with. Bake for 20 minutes in a moderate oven, and do not forget to keep the fish well moistened with the butter. Add a little lemon juice and grated nutmeg to the Dutch sauce if you wish; make it hot, and pour over the fish, which must be well drained from the butter. Garnish with parsley and cut lemon.

Time 30 minutes/Serves 4

DUTCH SAUCE FOR FISH

1/2 teaspoonful of flour
50g/2oz of butter
4 tablespoonfuls of vinegar
2 egg yolks
Juice of 1/2 a lemon
Salt to taste

Put all the ingredients, except the lemon juice, into a stewpan; set it on the heat, and keep continually stirring. When it has thickened, take it off, as it should not boil. If, however, it happens to curdle, strain the sauce through a sieve. Add the lemon juice and serve. Tarragon vinegar may be used instead of plain, and by many is considered far preferable.

Time 10 minutes to thicken/Serves 4

Lobster Salad

A hen lobster, boiled
Lettuces, endive, small salad greens
A little chopped beetroot
2 hard-boiled eggs
A few slices of cucumber

Wash and thoroughly dry the salad vegetables. Cut up the lettuces and endive, pour the dressing on them as below, add the small salad greens. Mix well together with the the lobster meat from the body and tail, having cut it up into nice square pieces, put half in the salad, and the other half reserve for garnishing. Separate the yolks from the whites of the hard-boiled eggs; chop the whites finely and rub the yolks through a sieve, and afterwards the coral from the inside. Arrange the salad on a dish, and garnish, first with a row of sliced cucumber, then with the pieces of lobster, the yolks and whites of the eggs, coral, and beetroot placed alternately, arranging in small separate bunches. A few crayfish or langoustines make a pretty garnish to lobster salad.
Time 1 hour/Serves 5-6

FRENCH DRESSING

Equal quantities of virgin olive oil and vinegar
1 teaspoonful of made mustard
2 egg yolks
Cayenne and salt to taste
1/4 teaspoonful of anchovy essence or paste

These ingredients should be mixed perfectly smooth to form a creamy-looking sauce.
Time 15 minutes/Serves 6

Whiting aux Fines Herbes

6 small whiting
A bunch of fresh Thyme, Parsley and Marjoram
50g/2oz of butter

Clean and skin the fish, fasten the tails in the mouths and lay them in a baking dish. Finely chop the herbs and sprinkle them over the fish. Add small pieces of butter, cover the dish and bake for 20 minutes in a hot oven. Turn the fish once or twice and serve hot with the butter and herbs poured over the finished dish.
Time 30 minutes/Serves 6

Toad in the Hole

675g/1¹/2lbs of rump steak
1 lamb's kidney
Pepper and salt to taste

For the batter

3 eggs
600ml/1 pint of milk
4 tablespoonfuls of flour
A pinch of salt

Cut up the steak and kidney into convenient sized pieces, and put them into a buttered pie dish, with a good seasoning of salt and pepper; mix the flour with a small quantity of milk at first, to prevent it being lumpy, then add the remainder with the 3 eggs, which should be well beaten. Add the salt, stir the batter for about 5 minutes and pour it over the steak. Place it in a moderately hot oven immediately, and bake for nearly 2 hours.
Time 2 hours/Serves 4-5

China Chilo

675g/1¹/2lbs of leg, loin or neck of mutton
2 onions
2 lettuces
450g/1lb of green peas
1 teaspoonful of salt and black pepper
150ml/¹/4 pint of water
100g/¹/4 lb of clarified butter
A little cayenne, when liked

Mince the above quantity of mutton, adding a little of the fat, also minced; put it into a stewpan with the remaining ingredients, previously shredding the lettuce and onion rather fine. Cover the stewpan, after the ingredients have been well stirred, and simmer for rather more than 2 hours. Serve in a dish, with a border of rice, the same as for curry.

Time 3 hours/Serves 3-4

Roast Leg of Lamb

2250-2700g/5-6lb leg or saddle of lamb
A little salt

Place the joint in a moderately hot oven, and baste well the whole time it is cooking. When nearly done make the oven very hot so that the joint acquires a nice brown colour. Take the joint out of the roasting pan and sprinkle a little fine salt over it. Add a little boiling water to the roasting juices and strain over the meat. Serve with mint sauce.

Time About 20 to 25 minutes per 450g/1lb/Serves 7 to 8

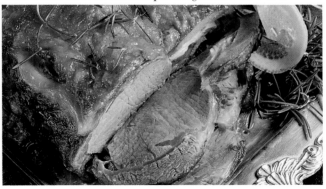

Pig's Trotters

4 pig's trotters
225g/8oz of pig's liver
225g/8oz of pig's heart
A thin slice of bacon
1 onion
1 blade of mace
6 peppercorns
3 or 4 sprigs of thyme
600ml/1 pint of gravy
Pepper and salt to taste
Thickening of butter and flour

Put the liver, heart and pig's trotters into a stewpan with the bacon, mace, peppercorns, thyme, onion and gravy, and simmer these gently for 20 minutes; then take out the heart and liver, and mince them very finely. Keep stewing the feet until quite tender, about 20 minutes, from the time that

they boiled up first, then put in the minced liver and heart, thicken the gravy with a little butter and flour, season with pepper and salt, and simmer over a gentle heat for 5 minutes, occasionally stirring. Dish the mince, split the feet, and arrange them round alternately with wedges of fried bread and pour the gravy in the middle.
Time Altogether 40 minutes/Serves 3-4

Veal à la Bourgeoise

900-1350g/2-3 lbs of loin or neck of veal
10-12 young carrots
A bunch of spring onions
2 slices of lean bacon
2 blades of mace, pounded
1 bunch of savoury herbs
Pepper and salt to taste
A few new potatoes
450g/1lb of shelled green peas
Bottled tomato sauce or mushroom ketchup to flavour
Butter

Cut the veal into cutlets, trim them and put the trimmings into a stewpan with a little butter; lay in the cutlets and fry them to a nice brown colour on both sides. Add the bacon, carrots, onions, mace, herbs and seasoning; pour in about 600ml/1 pint of boiling water and stew gently for 2 hours over a low heat. When done, skim off the fat, take out the herbs, and flavour the liquor with a little tomato sauce or mushroom ketchup. Have ready the peas and potatoes, boiled separately; put them with the veal and serve.
Time 2 hours/Serves 5-6

Fowl Pilaff

450g/1lb of Patna rice
50g/2oz butter
A plump fowl
2.2 litres/4 pints of stock or good broth
40 cardamom seeds
12g/¹/₂oz of coriander seeds
6g/¹/₄oz of cloves
6g/¹/₄oz of allspice
6g/¹/₄oz of mace
6g/¹/₄oz cinnamon
12g/¹/₂oz peppercorns
4 onions
6 thin slices of bacon
2 hard-boiled eggs

Well wash the rice, put it into a frying-pan with butter, and stir over a low heat until the rice is lightly browned. Truss the fowl, as for boiling, put it into a stewpan with the stock or broth; pound the spices and seed thoroughly in a mortar, tie them in a piece of muslin and put them in with the fowl. Let it simmer slowly until it is nearly done; then add the rice, which should stew until quite tender and almost dry; cut the onions into slices, sprinkle them with flour, and fry a nice brown colour without breaking them. Have ready the slices of bacon, rolled up and grilled, and the eggs. Lay the fowl in a dish, smother with the rice, after removing the spices, garnish with the bacon, fried onions, and hard-boiled eggs, cut into quarters, and serve very hot.

Time 30 minutes to boil a small fowl, with the rice/Serves 5-6

Jugged Hare

A hare
Forcemeat
675g/1¹/2lbs of shin of beef
225g/8oz of butter
1 onion
1 lemon
6 cloves
Pepper, cayenne and salt to taste
500ml/¹/2 pint of port
Flour

Skin, paunch and wash the hare, cut into pieces, dredge them with flour, and fry in butter. Have ready 900ml/1¹/2 pints of gravy, made from the above proportion of beef and thickened with a little flour. Put this into a jar; add the pieces of fried hare, an onion stuck with cloves, a lemon, peeled and cut in half, and a good seasoning of pepper, cayenne and salt. Cover the jar down tightly, put it up to the neck into a stewpan of boiling water and let it stew until the hare is quite tender, taking care to keep the water boiling. When nearly done, pour in the port and add a few balls of forcemeat; these must be fried or baked in the oven for a few minutes before they are put into the gravy. Serve with redcurrant jelly.

Time 3 to 4 hours; if the hare is old, allow 5 hours/Serves 7-8

Asparagus Pudding

225g/8oz of asparagus
4 eggs
2 tablespoonfuls of flour
1 tablespoonful of very finely minced ham
25g/1oz of butter
Pepper and salt to taste
Milk

Cut up the nice green tender parts of the asparagus spears and put them into a basin with the eggs, which should be well beaten, and the flour, ham, butter, pepper and salt. Mix all these ingredients well together, and moisten with sufficient milk to make the pudding of the consistency of thick batter. Put it into a buttered basin, tie it down tightly with a floured cloth, place it in boiling water, and let it boil for 2 hours; turn it out of the basin onto a hot dish, and pour plain melted butter round, but not over, the pudding.
Time 2 hours/Serves 4-5

Potatoes with Onions

450g/1lb potatoes, boiled in their skins
450g/1lb onions, finely minced
50g/2oz butter

While the potatoes are cooking, put the onions into a pan with the butter and cook them very gently until they are quite soft, this should take about 15 minutes. Peel and then mash the potatoes and then add and beat in the cooked onions and season to taste. Reheat before serving.
Time 30 minutes/Serves 8

Pease Pudding

675g/1¹/₂lbs of split peas
50g/2oz of butter
2 eggs
Pepper and salt to taste

Put the peas to soak overnight, and remove any that are discoloured. Tie them loosely in a clean cloth, leaving a little room for them to swell, and put them on to boil in cold water, allowing about 2 hours after the water has simmered up. When the peas are tender, take them up and drain; rub them through a colander with a wooden spoon, add the butter, eggs, pepper and salt, beat all well together for a few minutes, until the ingredients are well incorporated, then tie the mixture tightly in a floured cloth; boil the pudding for another hour, turn it out and serve very hot with Cumberland sausages.
Time 2 hours to boil the peas; 1 hour for the pudding/Serves 7-8

Broad Beans à la Poulette

1800g/4lbs of broad beans, shelled
300ml/¹/₂ pint of stock or broth
A small bunch of savoury herbs, including parsley
A small lump of sugar
1 egg yolk
150ml/¹/₄ pint of cream
Pepper and salt to taste

Take the young and freshly gathered beans and shell sufficient to make 675/1½lbs. Boil them in lightly salted water, until nearly done; then drain them and put them into a stewpan, with the stock, finely minced herbs and sugar. Stew the beans until they are tender, and the liquor has evaporated a little; then beat up the egg yolk with the cream and seasoning, add this to the beans, let the whole mixture get thoroughly hot and when on the point of simmering, serve.
Time 10 minutes to boil the beans; 15 minutes to stew them in the stock/Serves 4

Cauliflowers with Parmesan Cheese

2 or 3 small cauliflowers
Rather more than 300ml/½ pint of melted butter
2 tablespoonfuls of grated Parmesan cheese
50g/2 oz of butter
3 tablespoonfuls of breadcrumbs

Clean, trim and boil the cauliflowers, putting them in fast-boiling water with a little salt in it; drain them and dish them with the flowers standing upright. Have ready the melted butter; pour sufficient of it over the cauliflowers just to cover the top; sprinkle over this some of the Parmesan cheese and the breadcrumbs and drop on these the butter, which should be melted but not oiled. Brown in a hot oven or under the grill and pour round, but not over, the cauliflowers the remainder of the melted butter, with which should be mixed the rest of the grated Parmesan.
Time Altogether 30 minutes/Serves 8-10

Haricot Beans and Minced Onions

900g/2lbs of white haricot beans
4 medium-sized onions chopped
300ml/¹/2 pint of medium stock
Pepper and salt to taste
Flour

Fry the onions in butter until a light brown colour; dredge over them a little flour, and add the stock and a seasoning of pepper and salt. Have ready the haricot beans, well boiled and drained; put them with the onions and stock, mix all well together, and serve.
Time 2 hours/Serves 7-8

Stewed Cucumbers

6 cucumbers
3 medium-sized onions
Not quite 600ml/1 pint of white stock
Cayenne and salt to taste
2 egg yolks
A very little grated nutmeg

Peel and slice the cucumbers, take out the seeds, cut the onions into thin slices; put both vegetables into a stewpan with the stock and boil for 15 minutes, or longer should the cucumbers be very large. Beat up the yolks of the eggs, stir these into the cucumbers and add the cayenne, salt and grated nutmeg; bring to the point of boiling and serve with lamb chops or steaks.
Time Altogether 20 minutes/Serves 6-7

Stuffed Tomatoes

6 fairly large tomatoes, the tops removed
3 tablespoonfuls olive oil
2 large garlic cloves, crushed or finely chopped
1 medium onion, finely chopped
Salt and pepper
6 tablespoons fresh brown breadcrumbs
5 tablespoonfuls chicken stock
2 egg yolks

Remove the flesh from the tomatoes and rub through a
coarse sieve to remove the seeds. Then put into a small
pan with the oil, garlic, onion and seasoning, and cook gently
for 10 minutes. Remove and add 5 tablespoons of the breadcrumbs and the stock and blend thoroughly. Add the egg
yolks and mix again. Fill the tomatoes with the mixture,
sprinkle the remaining breadcrumbs over the top and bake at
190°C (375°F or Mark 5) for 10 minutes. Serve hot or cold.
Time 30 minutes/Serves 6

Cabinet or Chancellor's Pudding

38g/1¹/2 oz of candied peel
100g/4oz of currants
4 dozen sultanas
Sponge fingers or slices of sponge cake
4 eggs
600ml/1 pint of milk
Grated lemon rind
Grated nutmeg to taste
3 tablespoonfuls of caster sugar
Butter

Melt some butter and with it grease the mould or basin in which the pudding is to be boiled, taking care that it is buttered in every part. Cut the peel into thin slices and place these in a fanciful design at the bottom of the mould, and fill in the spaces between with currants and sultanas; then add a few sponge fingers or slices of sponge cake; dot melted butter on these and between each layer sprinkle a few currants. Proceed in this manner until the mould is nearly full; then flavour the milk with the nutmeg and grated lemon rind, add the sugar and stir it into the eggs, which should be well beaten. Beat this mixture for a few minutes, then strain it into the buttered mould, which should be quite full; tie a piece of buttered paper over it, and let it stand for 2 hours; then tie it down with a cloth, put it into boiling water and let it boil slowly for 1 hour. In taking it up, let it stand for a minute or two before the cloth is removed; then quickly turn it out of the mould and serve with sweet sauce.
Time 1 hour/Serves 5-6

Canary Pudding

The weight of 3 eggs in caster sugar
The weight of 3 eggs in butter
The weight of 2 eggs in flour
The rind of 1 small lemon
3 eggs

Melt the butter to a liquid state, but do not allow it to oil; stir into this the sugar and finely minced lemon peel and gradually dredge in the flour, keeping the mixture well stirred. Whisk the eggs, add these to the pudding, beat all the ingredients until thoroughly blended and put them into a buttered mould or basin covered with buttered paper and a cloth. Boil for 2 hours and serve with sweet sauce.
Time 2 hours/Serves 4-5

Carrot Pudding

225g/8oz of fresh breadcrumbs
100g/4oz of suet
100g/4oz of raisins
350g/12oz of fresh boiled carrots
100g/4oz of currants
75g/3 oz of caster sugar
3 eggs
Milk
Grated nutmeg

Boil the carrots until tender enough to mash to a pulp; add the other ingredients, and moisten with sufficient milk to make the pudding the consistency of thick batter. If you wish to boil the pudding, put the mixture into a buttered basin, tie it down with a cloth and boil for about 2 hours; you can bake it by putting it into a pie dish and bake in a moderate oven for nearly 1 hour; turn it out, strew sifted sugar over it and serve.

Time 2 hours to boil, 1 hour to bake/Serves 5-6

Bakewell Pudding

100g/4oz of puff pastry
5 eggs
150g/6oz of caster sugar
100g/4oz of butter
25g/1oz of ground almonds
Jam

Cover a dish with the paste, rolled thin and put over this a layer of any kind of jam, 12mm/^{1}/$_2$ inch thick; put the yolks of the eggs into a basin with the white of one and beat these well; add the sugar, the butter, which should be melted, and the almonds; beat all together until well mixed, then pour it into the dish over the jam and bake for 1 hour in a moderate oven.

Time 1 hour/Serves 4-5

Rhubarb Tart

225g/8oz of puff pastry
5 large sticks of rhubarb
100g/4oz of sugar

Make the puff paste, line the edges of a deep pie dish with it and wash, wipe and cut the rhubarb into pieces about 25mm/1 inch long. Should the rhubarb be old and tough, string it, that is to say pare off the outside skin. Pile the fruit high in the dish, as it shrinks very much in the cooking; put in the sugar, cover with a lid with puff paste, ornament the edges and bake in a brisk oven for 40 minutes. When the tart is nearly baked, brush it over with the white of an egg beaten to a stiff froth, then sprinkle on it some sifted sugar and put it in the oven to set the glaze. A small quantity of lemon juice and a little of the peel minced, will add an improvement to the flavour of rhubarb tart.
Time 1 hour/Serves 4-5

Vol-au-vent of Fresh Strawberries

450g/1lb of puff pastry
450g/1lb of freshly gathered strawberries
Sugar to taste
Whipped cream

Make a vol-au-vent case by the following method: roll out the puff paste to a thickness of 25mm/1 inch; using a fluted cutter, press out a round of paste about 150mm/ 6 inches across. With a sharp knife, make a slight incision in the paste all round the top, about 25mm/1 inch from the edge, which, when baked, will form the lid. Put the vol-au-vent into a hot oven for about 30 minutes; when nearly done, brush the paste over with the white of an egg, then sprinkle on it some caster sugar and put it back in the oven to set the glaze; when golden in colour, take it out of the oven, instantly remove the lid where it was marked and detach all the pastry from the centre. Just before serving, fill it with the strawberries, adding sufficient sugar to sweeten them nicely. Place a few spoonfuls of whipped cream on top and serve. Time 40 minutes/Serves 4-6 (or make individual cases using smaller rounds of puff pastry).

Pears à l'Allemande

6-8 pears
Water
Sugar
50g/2oz butter
1 egg yolk
12g/½oz gelatine

Peel and cut the pears and steep them in cold water to prevent them turning brown; put them into a saucepan with sufficient cold water to cover them and simmer them, with the butter and enough sugar to sweeten them nicely, until tender. Brush them over with the yolk of an egg, sprinkle them with sifted sugar and arrange them on a dish. Dissolve the gelatine in the cooking syrup, boil it up quickly for about 5 minutes, strain it over the pears and let it remain until set. The syrup may be coloured with a little cochineal, which would very much improve the appearance of the dish. Time 20 minutes to stew the pears; 5 minutes for the syrup/ Serves 6-8